This Planet Neighborhood

This Planet Neighborhood

Poems by

Priscilla Denby

© 2025 Priscilla Denby. All rights reserved.
This material may not be reproduced in any form, published,
reprinted, recorded, performed, broadcast,
rewritten, or redistributed without
the explicit permission of Priscilla Denby.
All such actions are strictly prohibited by law.

Cover design by Shay Culligan
Cover image by Priscilla Denby
Author photo by J. V. Jones

ISBN: 978-1-63980-999-8
Library of Congress Control Number: 2025937994

Kelsay Books
502 South 1040 East, A-119
American Fork, Utah 84003
Kelsaybooks.com

*For my family and friends,
especially Anthony, Arlyn, Paula, and Geoff,
and all who helped sub rosa and otherwise—
you know who you are*

Acknowledgments

Grateful acknowledgment is made to the editors of the journals and anthologies who first published the following poems. The poems, sometimes in earlier versions, appeared as follows:

Indiana Writes: "These Birds," "The Next Time We Meet"
Poetry Northwest: "Ribbed Cages" as "Tight Cages"
Quarry: "Mountain Stream"

Many thanks to Phyllis Repicky, Andrea Ferentinos, Laura Baum-Parr, and dear Maggie, Margaret Downing, for reading drafts, and to my superb editor, April Ossmann, who envisioned a future for this manuscript.

I'm indebted to my Bloomington buddies who feasted on poetry and music every Sunday at Ruth Stone's home: George Ella and Steve Lyon, Barry Childs, Rory and Marilyn Holscher, Deborah Campbell, Geoff Rips, Michael Allen. Such abiding inspiration.

Kudos and oodles of thanks to my dear friend, author J.V. Jones, for her technical and artistic expertise and advice on all things publishing.

Many thanks to Paul Jones for helping design the cover.

Teaching English for more than twenty-five years has given me hours of pleasure discussing poetry with colleagues and students, and I am indebted to all.

I am exceeding grateful to everyone at Kelsay Books. I am so lucky that *This Planet Neighborhood* found a home with such remarkable people.

Contents

I

A Man Yawning	17
George Washington Returns for the Bicentennial	19
This Day That Began Elsewhere	20
What I Understand	21
Twins	22
Meadowfield	24
The Man Whose Dog Was Taken by a Coyote	26
Xylophones of Broken Glass	27
Strains of Light	28
Instructions for Meeting a Coyote	31

II

Driving to Work	35
Ribbed Cages	37
Crescent Springs and After	38
Id to Ego	41
Axis Mundi	43
The Next Time We Meet	45
A Poet Going Blind	46
One Street in This Planet Neighborhood	48
We Remember It Differently	50
To Bill, a Friend I Haven't Written	53
The Vagaries of Light	55
Mountain Stream	57
Our Neck of the Woods	58
Enough Music to Dance By	60

III

Wild Light on Water	63
Spare Deserts	64
New Parents	65
Every Survival	67
The Possibility of Evening	68
In the Somewhere Somehow Somewhen	69
No Discovery Without Music	70
This Bed	72
Sailing Mission Bay	74
Summer 2020	75
The House Where I Live	76
These Birds	78
The Nearest While	79
Fritz	80
Witness	81
Where We Find Ourselves	83
Notes	87

*Would a bird build its nest if it did not have
its instinct for confidence in the world?*

—Gaston Bachelard

*Tomorrow morning before we depart,
I intend to land and see
what can be found in the neighborhood.*

—Christopher Columbus

I

A Man Yawning

As we stand awaiting
a light change,

my fellow pedestrian
coughs, making room

in his chest's lowest rungs
for morning air he breathes

into his lungs like I might
drink champagne, air he swallows

like a world so whole,
he barely gets his mouth around it.

A woman jaywalks toward us,
wearing headset, watch, and wires

sufficient to study
the gravitational laxity

of Jupiter's moons
or supersonic screeching

of katydids mating—
her eyes gone to the audio balm,

losing the chance to *tsk-tsk,*
or smile with me at his maw,

or nod to say we are neighbors—
and this man, this affirmation

of self-sustaining life,
this prehensile yawn

and its contagion,
is the one required

reflex keeping this planet
neighborhood alive.

George Washington Returns for the Bicentennial

It was the body poised motionless
in a motion-filled boat,
some to-do over throwing a silver dollar.

It was the body unfinished, ghosted below
the frame of Gilbert Stuart's vision,
the face rising from the canvas fog

so often gazing up from my palm,
one I wanted to switch
to the well-heeled Grant or Franklin.

But there he stood, coin in hand,
looking for something—
a general store, where one dollar

equals four tomatoes, a sack of flour,
three gils of rice, two pounds of pork,
and a loaf of bread—or a tavern,

somewhere to sit and ravish a pint,
a place to shuck his boots and lay his head,
just as if war never happened to it.

I leaned over to whisper to him
that things had changed,
that there was no need to cross

the ice-floed Delaware by rickety boat,
he'd find a welcoming hotel right up the road,
with phones and electricity, a nation with states

he'd never heard of still celebrating his name,
his portrait on every quarter and dollar,
whether he wanted it or not.

This Day That Began Elsewhere

This day that began elsewhere,
well-travelled, a stranger
with good credentials,
four and a half billion years old—
arrives unannounced, as if knowing
I've been awaiting its light spores
spritzing my face,
the supposed windows of my soul.

Now summer's nowhere but
where I sit, legs stretched out,
bare feet propping up the porch
of this old house in a space
called *Indiana,*
a mote in infinity's eye.

I try reading, to let words
think for me,
while days turn like pages of a book
I hope one day to translate
into even one truth I understand.

Maybe this day will take my hand,
and wing me to a view of Earth
that doesn't end in darkness—

I lean deeper into the day's embrace,
sink into the warmth,
the resolute pulse
of its winning ways—

the sun has been a steady sweetheart,
but I hear the breakup is coming.

What I Understand

Love, ocean is a wish repeated:
wherever you go,

it has traveled there before.
Sometimes when it seems asleep,

or without answers,
the ocean's lip curves—

it tells what it means
to be free of crops and houses,

its sound, whole civilizations
crumbling down.

I am the fisherman's house
perched at the water's edge,

a trawler in waiting,
squatter gulls on its hull.

You are the questions
arched into answers

that never touch shore,
each wave taunting this gull,

floating each boat
like the sea's last bottle.

Twins

I

Born connected to a rope
strong enough to pull our own ark.

We learned to tie shoes
on the very same day.

Wherever I stand on the planet,
I'm pulled tight

to your center,
our hands and minds twined

like redwoods'
underground knots.

II

Please spell your name.
P, then *R* articulated more slowly,
the aged, German doctor's hand

retracing its work,
as if a bountiful sound spill
needed clean-up,

I then *S,*
time enough for birds' nest building
or a Sleepy Hollow nap,

with the *C* positioned in my lips,
a race horse lunging at the gate,
Slow down, please,

the seismic *I-L-L-A*
ended with the prescription
in my hand—

Why are you laughing?—
her turn to be gently irked.
You wrote my twin's name.

Impossible,
I wrote every letter
you said.

My sister, un-bodied,
a thousand miles away,
capturing this woman's ear,

recalibrating causal reality,
leaving me wondering,
What was Phyllis trying to say?

Meadowfield

The beauty of near redundancy
thrives in Meadowfield,
where free-range grasses, ferns,
sedges, shrubs, and wildflowers populate
open spaces hailed with glossy praise
in the city's tourist ads,

but today I learned Oxford has X'd
meadow from the children's
dictionary, in favor of *broadband, blog,
sidebar,* and *cut and paste,*

an amalgam
of every meadow
you've strolled, each step
holding imagination's light,

Elvira Madigan racing through
weeds' unkempt beauty,
Mozart in the wind, her lover
ripe with waiting,
whole species of flowery words
native to Austin and Bronte,
Catherine and Heathcliff
meeting amid blooming heather,
Jane and Edward chasing dragonflies
on Thornfield's lawn—

the lexical erosion hits me
like a glacial understanding of weight
and influence sped up by millennia,

while the meadow meanders
to bloom undercover,
hardy as the genus
of human memory,
preserving nature,
dictionary and nomenclature free.

The Man Whose Dog Was Taken by a Coyote

greets me—his words,
like Monet's rolling hills,
lead light and color into the distance,
till they mesh beyond the time frame
where we stand conversing,
two bodies stuck for a moment
in this one Earthly intersection
of space and time,
while rogue planets traverse the void,
and his eyes lock
on a realm of existence
fathoms of light years
into his own interior.

I, the Mars Rover, a tiny speck
exploring its surface,
my mechanical, *Hi how are you?*
Nice day, isn't it?
a titanium arm trying
to retrieve a rock
or a bit of sand to bring back
to Earth, to study
and determine his location,
how untold eons have changed him,
if his language has evolved past
the phonemes we once shared,
this man barely sensing my two pups,
alive, eager to restart the walk,
aware of the molten depths of his grief.

Xylophones of Broken Glass

Uncle, you played every instrument,
arranged pieces for Tommy Dorsey
and the Big Bands in Swing's heyday,

and once I saw you traveling piano keys,
eyes flying to the ether,
bulky fingers adrift in fields of light,
flickering one shy note, then
another, enticing stars to awaken
a summer's evening,

but I never really understood
that moment
till the pickle jar crashed like a cymbal
on the pavement in Ashtabula—

When out of the literal blue,
the wind showed up
mimicking birdsong,
fluting tremolos,
riffing xylophones
of broken glass,
as a timpani of lower octave trucks
rumbled the highway—

and right on the flamboyant
upbeat you trumpeted,
*This Could Be the Start
of Something Big,*
in your best Steve Allen voice,
scoring and forever arranging
the musical undertones of our existence,
the infinite variations
of our fleeting wonder.

Strains of Light

I

A young man jumped from the pool
palming something very small,
and with a first grader's attention,
scratched a hole and buried it,
patting the mound with reverence.

Was it a seed, a start-up oak or pine
soon to dominate forest brethren,
the next wolf-tree of mythology?
A time capsule Guinness World Records
will honor for its minuscule scale,
GPS instructions from an internet
scavenger hunt, or a love note
to someone he dared not approach?

When he looked up, I smiled.
What did you just do?
I buried a bee.
Alive or dead?
Dead. They do a lot for us, you know.

I had just crushed a bee,
sparing my pups a Hercules
with poisoned arrow
agonizing in his last throes.

My lips curved in the not-quite rueful
half-smile, half-frown
unable to be reined in or reconciled,
or redacted from our genome

as I thanked God
for these competing strains of light,

the sole force we can muster
to pulverize AI,
the enemy combatant embedded
like a journalist in a military tank,
about to breach the human cell's
membrane,
delicate as the young man's nod
before he walked away.

II

When I saw the young man again,
kneeling, cradling something
in the altar of his hands,
I asked,
Another?
Yes.

I told him about killing the bee,
that light clashing with light
is humanity's
slap on the bottom cry—

and me, clenching a pen
the way birthing women
once bit on a stick,

bearing this poem,
limbs still trying to swim
from the womb,
fingers foraging the air,
words beyond reach.

When he asked to read it,
I knew I'd leave
its folded parchment skin
on his doorstep,
confident in his tenderness.

Instructions for Meeting a Coyote

If you're walking your dogs
and spot a coyote,

puff up your nimbus,
stick out your best predator's chest.

If you have three or more hands,
un-pocket your air whistle,

bear spray, or wolf pee,
or trust your luck

locating the stones
the earth will provide

as your weapons of choice,
while you un-harness your voice

to scream *Help!*
to summon an unoccupied god,

or un-sheep the world at large—
or do anything else

your brain can sapien—
like trying to be friends,

or making amends
for stealing their territory.

I hear reciting Ferlinghetti
will make these beasts flee

in fear of catching
your insanity.

A coyote of the considerate ilk
will wait till your flailings stop

and you lift your baton
to let the orchestration begin—

but if you now meet plural coyotes
rubbernecking this takedown

of your presence
versus the virtual world

where most of us live,
hope to God for neighbor Neanderthals

who practice by instinct,
instruction, or personal induction,

the long-in-the-tooth coyotes' truth:
that the pack is the only way

to get the real world's work done
and done.

II

Driving to Work

I round the highway's bend
same as yesterday
and the day before, and see
a drake, his mate,
and seven ducklings.

This landscape holds
no ocean or river,
no water to test
a webbed foot

or its triathalonic feat—
the intra second navigation
of air and land and water.

Is this a new duck breed,
current stars of Darwin-at-large,
that makes them flop down on macadam
so close to the speeding cars?

Have they adopted a soon-to-be reality,
the Tesla of their ilk?
Were they hand-picked
for a fowl experiment
measuring the misery
bred through human sprawl?

Did they fall prey
to a shady Airbnb?
or just stupidity,
staking territory no other
species challenges or wants?

Curiously, not one has been killed yet,
though I saw a hen
lying on her side,
flapping at me,
as if to ask how I could pass,
as she mounted a last ditch
attempt to reach the Hudson,
or some beginner's pond nearby,

making me avert my eyes
and continue driving,
on my way to make
what we call *a living*.

Ribbed Cages

Charity lives in Vermont and has no bones,
born a silken sack, carrying her name
in a skin diffuse as sunlight touching sand.

Her birth left her mother and the landscape nearly
unmarked. Post partum, steers continue chewing cuds
like old men, and mountains still bump the clouds

like winning athletes bumping chests. The townsfolk,
Vermont pines in their spines, have never seen her,
only heard tell of wheelbarrows of marrow imported

from Chester and closer. They sink, rigid ships,
in her garden. Petunias blush hemoglobin, marigolds
no longer move. Bones grow there—stone bones,

radish bones, wheat bones, and dogs have begun
to sprout. But Charity, toothless as a wave of starlight,
flows beyond the garden, streaming like the water

that weaned Noah's ark from earth and drifted
continents. She surges deep as the Pacific,
past men and women in ribbed cages.

Crescent Springs and After

I

Wind and sun syncopate,
    jazz of April, gingham fields.

Your shadow happens
    on petals and branches,

then fastens on me
    like a lover.

Like the moon,
    your smile promises

to shine its gorgeous
    light forever.

In its gentle curve,
    I stake a claim

in a cradle of civilization
    unknown to maps,

teeming with April's
    nectar,

more than enough for us—
    and a nod

to the peacocks
    of May,

lovely in their sassy
    ignorance.

II

Stripped of etiquette
   or explanation,

you landed on
   my doorstep,

one clean-shaven
   August night.

We skinned the hours
   with long even glances,

but the air massed
   in your corner,

a storm building,
   till I couldn't

speak your name,
   nor places tied to it.

You said you liked
   one-line poems—

I remember little else—
   your smile swirling

over icy scotch,
   a scythe razing the room.

III

I mattered
   like a rainbow at night.

I hear your footsteps
   on the doorstep

you do not find,
   as a backlog of dreams

burns beneath a cropless
   harvest moon—

it mocks me with its cold,
   second-hand light,

illuminating your name—
   a one-line poem

I must still eclipse
   from memory.

Id to Ego

We have met in darkness,
in silence and whining,
in everyday wrangling,

so you know me well:
I am the absence of stars
on a summer evening.

All day, the valley lifts
trees, streams, houses still
as August wheat

to better see the sun,
drifting field flowers
in unnamed constellations,

maps for the skies
I'll never travel,
recitations for night

as Earth rolls
into its own shadow,
and welcome relief—

a sleep much thicker
than your skin, deeper
than your understanding—

but you break through,
ever day's champion,
heliotroping towards morning,

scattering seeds of light
in the widest wind,
shining like lost secrets.

Axis Mundi

*Before the heart of the universe
began beating in clocks,
the whole fish-cold Earth,
still unseeded with ships,
swam the dark fathoms
of Numbakula's womb.*

Unwrapping from sleep, I opened a door
that swung like a pendulum
between us. Neither of us
meant anything by it. Neither of us meant.

*The very first spring,
his belly swelled to explosion,
spilling colors until he was
pale as the farthest stars,
thin as the life-spine he lifted
from the trunk of a gum tree.*

He just stood, bannerless, coat-tugging,
begging recognition—a strange child
with mud-tracked smiles
where the world crept across his face
which he tried to wipe
with Grand Central air.
Where is his mother? I can only guess
she is no one real.

*He unfolded the sleeping Ancestors,
spun their songs, gods,
fertile lands, round them,
in the center, the sacred pole.*

His eyes are round enough
for the Earth and sky to hide in,
to rhyme the speechless sea.
He can lure the wind at whim,
skip dreams he doesn't like.

See the kauwa-auwa bend,
how it curls day into night,
gives grasses direction,
shows paths the Alchilpa must travel
to center the world.

My hand tight-circles this little traveler's:
a transparent oyster, a foundling pearl.
Apprehensions surface the way tiny fish
whisper bubbles proving they exist.
Kidnapper? I am no harm.
Together we will be a home.

Already silk echoes on the mountain.
Daybreak yeasts a savory noon.
Morning glories open the twilight.
My *axis mundi* runs with the world
astring, no longer a stray.

The Next Time We Meet

I'll stand in the crossroads
you make
when you enter a room.
Clouds will bluster overhead
like men who have seen
too much water.
All the wrong moments of our lives
will pour down.

You will not smile or kiss:
but say you've been courting
persimmons,
your tongue's away on vacation;
you'll toss me hellos
and other empty packages
to open again, again,
in the unwrapped night.

Please be fair. I am trying
every magic:
I'll dance if you're thirsty;
pray if you need food;
I will untie my shoelaces
if you're about to give birth.

A Poet Going Blind

Ruth sits in the wicker chair
grown thick in her farmhouse
kitchen,

words simmering
from the vast bellied pot
on the stove,

strolling imagination
and memory's trees,
some still green,

some now reddening
the mountains with autumn's
advent, a feast capped

by great-granddaughter
Odette, fluttering
across the floor

like a dragonfly
dipping its toes in water,
sun dancing its wings.

Ruth bathes like a stone
in that stream,
making its rivulets sing,

as branches' nave hosts
birds' catechism,
her question answered,

imagining Odette's
future words, as a wedge
of trumpeter swans

in flight, soft-lit
by the waning moon,
still shining in her room—

a vision which
arrests the night,
arrests the night.

One Street in This Planet Neighborhood

At eighty-five, with a coif
to die for, Reyna can't recall

who styles her hair,
but sits on the poolside bench

engaged in a ballerina's
barre work,

palms and fingers navigating the air,
arms reciting the muscled pleasure

of a swan's rippling neck, each tendon
reaching its grace potential.

Up the block, gentleman Herald
plays Lazarus, slow-raising

a '55 Plymouth Plower from the dead,
part by expensive part,

his smile mirrored in every polish,
all sweating body in summer heat,

as he ages in place, content
to await its second coming.

Next door in his friend Sal's
open garage, Lionel trains run

on multiple tracks through villages
of circumscribed time and place,

while fleeting thoughts never quite arrive,
like stopped trains awaiting late connections

with other engines and cars,
as the stars wheel unseen above

this planet neighborhood,
where his fellows recast earlier days,

various degrees away from the void
some deny and others imagine—

what goes on beyond the skilled edge
of the mortician's ministrations.

We Remember It Differently

We both remember
she opened her eyes,

acknowledged our presence,
tried to grab the oxygen mask,

*Mom, the doctors want you
to keep this in place—*

a twin on either side,
holding a hand in comfort

and restraint, two women
made aware of their sisterhood,

mourning its declining source,
its potential severability.

I remember how at the end
she slowly raised one shoulder,

as grudges, redacted secrets,
unkempt thoughts, valentines

never sent, eighty-nine years'
sediment shed, spirit lifted

with the magnitude
of her breath,

then the other shoulder,
raised and released,

then both flying together—like a pilot
circling for the landing,

weather good, traffic cleared,
landing strip prepared,

shoulders squared
to greet her Maker—

No, Phyllis remembers,
she never raised both shoulders,

she tented one, then the other,
nothing afterwards—

Phyllis insists it happened the way
mother cooked our breakfasts,

fed the cat before the dog,
both before the parakeet,

finally sitting to sip
lukewarm coffee in peace—

we remember it differently,
such a small gargantuan thing—

but I choose to see both shoulders
rise in unison,

her Atlas weight
released,

the decrescendo's final harmonic note,
bows gently eking out every vibrato,

leaving the audience,
seats bolted to the floor,

straining at their tethers,
eyes on instruments

still lifted, awaiting direction,
the baton paused aloft,

ears hearing beyond
earthly capability,

her pure filament of music
reaching the eternal,

leaving our *Not sure
what we saw and heard,*

our wondering *Is it over?*
our hoping *It's not.*

To Bill, a Friend I Haven't Written

Instead of stealing a poem,
I'll rent a cathedral-ceilinged one,
with colossal skylights,

and room enough
for bear-shaped clouds
to tumble in spring fields

among Wordsworth's daffodils.
Grand staircases will flow
endlessly as Whitman,

library nooks hide,
shy as Dickinson's secrets,
and doors open

the dappled worlds
Hopkins found
between words.

I need this house to write you:
its attic trunks caching folded years,
its stacks of unused words.

When I hold them to the light,
what's faded will brighten,
the way morning slips

back into a tree.
I will send you this house
by express mail,

its windows like packages of sky
that keep arriving.
You will be the river sliding

like sap from the mountain,
the rocks, grass, and fields unfolding
so the house can center the hill.

The Vagaries of Light

What interests me,
as I write in the light's halo,

is the shadow hugging my hand's
underside,

unintended yet resolute,
a loyal maid in waiting,

a subterranean railroad
for my sleight of hand misdeeds,

darkness cloaking words
as I splay them naked on the page.

This is a perfectly respectable
function of light,

casting the shadow that will
mute the page enough to see it.

For too long we've slandered
the shadow as evil or needy,

a sycophant without care
of reputation, or unnecessary,

we've forgotten how shade
saves lives in withering sun,

how we welcome dark's sweet relief
and healing in sleep.

Perhaps we overvalue shadow's
parasitic host:

we all know how the headlight
or match lit in the fog,

a concentrated fist of light,
makes it harder to see,

or at least illuminates the obvious fact
that light doesn't solve everything,

though I cannot deny its most
beautiful certainties—

its unparalleled trifecta
of sun, moon, and starlight,

how it shines up as well as down,
mimics water to flow around

whatever's in its way,
creates shadow,

or positions itself
so no shadow takes hold—

vagaries of light
dependent, in turn,

on those
of every creature on Earth.

Mountain Stream

To be a stream is to find
sun, leaves, bluefish,
footprints inside you;
the colors loosed
when an otter swims,
oak roots aching to travel.
A stream is the celebration
of rain, ceremony to keep
the mountain whole.

To be a stream is to serenade
the early air,
float woodlarks' songs
where they want to go.
Lakes would climb
up mountains if they could,
be the stream itself,
feel the sky nudge
like a deer come to drink.

Mother, you've become
the mountain, giving rushing water
its font, and its pathway
through the world.

To think of you is to shine
like the stream and know why
it shines, to know why
I am never alone on the mountain.

Our Neck of the Woods

Last century, when the moon
first felt a human touch,
Jean Ritchie strummed chords-in-waiting
for the ballad she planned to sing,
when someone asked:
*What's the most beautiful thing
you ever saw?*

She didn't hesitate:
*I was lying in the grass
beneath an apple tree,
clouds shape-shifting
behind its feast of blossoms,
when a continent of bluebirds
landed in the branches.*

Did she mention the clouds parted
to let the sun create a shimmer
of blue,
how it infused her?

I don't remember,
yet I have lain
in her mind,
the cool grass holding me,
each bird bringing me
its untapped blue,
its infinite promise.

In my neighborhood
of infinite promise,
the beautiful is subject
to the sun's whimsy—

if it spotlights a gecko
arching back like a dancer,
or the green lounging on the hill
where a Jacaranda flouts
its gifted purple,
or a beleaguered, wafting mist
holds the light
so it transforms a trashcan
into the solid glistening
of Tutankhamun art.

Today, a young man and woman
with quiet clothes and words,
walk together, sun following,
each holding a cup of coffee.

They harbor a sweet air,
as if I stand on a wharf
looking at sun-brushed sea,
and the water is happy.

It washes over me,
as unknowingly they walk in step,
unaware of the singular beauty
they create,
their synchrony of being.

Enough Music to Dance By

Dearest Niece,
If you are the ocean's rising tides
twirling and leaping,
catching the cadence of light
falling across sands, its waves
turning and tuning the earth,
making enough music to dance by—

we are the shore for the harmonics
you bring—what's sure and true
and will not stop, what's deepest
inside everything—
to hold you is to pass along the dance,
to revel in the Earth's internal spin.

III

Wild Light on Water

Wild light on water, a flicker of *yes,*
synaptic spark of all life to be—
as life's reach extends, the promise of less

natural chaos, serendipitous mess,
the fertile birthing of volcanic seas,
wild light on water, a flicker of *yes,*

less raw pluck, errant seed of most progress
and truth—the lambent touch, the bare-skinned knee—
as life's reach extends, the promise of less

unmapped emotion, to feel or express,
sparking vast shifts in the heart's galaxy—
wild light on water, a flicker of *yes,*

no whorl of guess, lush ambiguousness,
nuance—the crux of our humanity—
as life's reach extends, the promise of less:

our minds lie fallow, our hearts beat bloodless—
glad slaves of virtual technocracy—
wild light on water, a flicker of *yes,*
as life's reach extends, the promise of (more and more) less.

Spare Deserts

I am lonely for you tonight.
The wind is bare,

hugging cold my shoulders.
It is not enough.

God himself stands naked
without handshakes or soothing words.

A million severed cacti
puncture the black shroud covering me,

stars like endless pinpricks
of panoramic pain.

Yesterday's rain has turned
to tumbleweeds in my throat,

so I cannot speak
your name.

Your silence could erode
gold or silver or the sun.

I'm not rich, though
I have deserts to spare,

but I have a jungle heart,
lush enough for loving.

New Parents

I

For months, a strong wind
with nowhere to settle.
The tree that took it in
as branches' breath,
now cradles the sun.

Birds begin there,
calls colliding
like wind and rain,
songs warding them off
like prayer—birth

is this music,
conducting you, belly-warm
as the bud-flooded oak,
round as the anniversary rings
it wears,
roots tunneling love-deep
and further,
chords of the melody you bear.

II

You wait like the ocean
waiting to hold a boat,

a boat waiting
to float a life to shore,

an ocean expanding,
forming new beaches,

reshaping continents,
like a god you never imagined

you'd find inside,
responsible

for a whole new world
in need of sea,

of the music
new life makes,

your son new to sunlight,
but not to singing,

his every incantation
an invocation to your futures.

Every Survival

Light unfurls the garden, flame by flower,
the universe relies on the hand that tends
crocus then iris, hour by hour,

as the cosmos bursts in celestial showers,
of planets and protons, beginnings on end,
light unfurls the garden, flame by flower,

so petals express ineffable power,
as does one green leaf and all it intends—
crocus then iris, hour by hour,

but ceded within this inviolate bower,
hate blazes so bright that darkness portends—
light unfurls the garden, flame by flower.

Still, where those scourged by civil wars cower,
as bud turns to flower, may foe become friend—
crocus then iris, hour by hour.

Extend the open hand, the heart-held *our*—
on this Earth's every survival depends:
light unfurls the garden, flame by flower,
crocus then iris, hour by hour—

The Possibility of Evening

You would unlatch the hovering sky,
rocket its hypersonic bluster,
its secret inner worlds,

explore galactic fun houses
with comet trails and planetary spins,
ride Neil Armstrong's shoulders

in astral parades, pilot your own ship
between interstellar songs,
the music of the spheres to guide you—

arms linked with Orion, you would
hunt galaxies and missing asteroids,
notching your belt with stars.

I stand beside you, every unmapped
galaxy spinning madly within me,
waiting for you to revisit Earth,

the basic geography of you and me,
riding the light together,
splicing time and space.

Unaware, you ponder the possibility
of evening, as we watch the sky move
the Midwest to the Rockies.

In the Somewhere Somehow Somewhen

Since the birthing of stars—
in the somewhere somehow somewhen—
since rays took wing from their nests,

and fledgling planets grew
and took hold,
and galaxies, rich with time's gossamer,
spun webs of gold
filigreed with particles of promise—

light has been traveling,
to you, to us.

Holding you, your newborn heat
cradling me in the comfort
of one more generation,
I feel the generosity of light,
warmth untold,
time demystified.

Dear nephew, seed of light,
our shining sweeps the horizon.

No Discovery Without Music

Things more precious to Isabella
than jewels:
    Columbus had a grand staff
    with a thousand clarinets,
    Balboa as many bassoons,
        crossing oceans of scales,
        following birds' orchestrations,
        and whale-spouted tunes.

Nature's melodic pings chimed
in Newton's soul:
    clouds tapping mountains,
    apples ringing orchards
    like bells,
        drumming his back
        and head,
        as he lazed upon the knoll.

Electrons danced in Einstein's brain
all day long:
    when he heard life's endless refrain,
    from here and now to now and then,
    no music ever lost—
        his hair stood on end
        in six dimensions
        and he burst into song.

Musk dreams the sacred chants
morning makes on Mars:
    winds whipping up manic riffs
    of sands percussing
    rocks and submerged seas
        into microscopic
        rhapsodies
        that bellow to the stars.

He'll croon Earth's greatest hits,
with voices lost in war, after sickness,
in an ex-lover's drawer,
as he plants the flag of music,
the maestro of human discovery.

This Bed

This bed goes back further
than flowers.

Forget the scent of magnolias
that curls us ivory,

closer to moonlit sleep.
If you close your eyes,

petals flee their centers
like birds their nests.

We are birds migrating back
to a beautiful beginning:

ocean, then light, gardens
that grew from them only—

we lie in that ocean,
naked of land and time,

your hands rediscovering
the sweep of my body,

tides of hurts, reprisals,
unmet desires

receding,
until I am

the bodiless whisper
of a white wave

arched to sunlight—
you,

the seed
of Babylonian green.

Sailing Mission Bay

This wind is too weak
to make apples fall:
in an orchard it would settle
for petals,
or sailing a single leaf
toward summer's end.

But butter-thick air
chameleons in your hands,
spinning itself into wind-webs
that net your sails
and free us from shore,

a flag waving over ocean,
the land offering
what it usually only trades
for work: houses, corn,
roads that root cities to towns—
though we don't need
to own it
with more than our eyes
and memories—

Power gleaned from air,
your way—
helm parting water
that smoothes again
like a dolphin's fin,
a gentle meeting of friends.

Summer 2020

The day after my dinner party,
I see the generals have been by again,
to remind me of my duty.
Inside I find un-swept debris,
evidence of five-star hubris
plastered against the walls.

Outside sparrows align
with bare tree branches,
a camouflaged militia.
I feel them, the way a woman
raises children to go to war.

I see my friends whose work
was taken away,
let down by everyone
and no one in particular,
it's for them I put the feeder in this tree,
upsetting sparrows' maneuvers,
persuading them to shed their loyalties,
leave the generals behind.

For them I restore lost sustenance,
seed outside and this dough inside,
awakened in my hands,
pillowing to a loaf,
all its promises rising.

The House Where I Live

Everywhere walls allowed space
to fit a bureau or human,

but now,
these vein-thin rafters

sapped by ancestral winters,
too weak to keep

windows apart,
lean toward each other,

recalling pre-indentured days,
when free-flowing

xylem and phloem
conditioned trees to stand

shoulder to shoulder,
forest-worthy,

bearing the sweet brunt
of wrens' ceaseless chatter,

as branches muscled ice storms,
testing their tensile strength.

Now bulky weather
incites them—

the wind's heft,
snow squirreling inside,

compressing wood grains.
I try talking to oak, walnut,

pine, and they bark back
with sass I thought

they'd left behind:
the floor splits, slanting

toward the Earth's axis,
a window slams shut,

its preferred modality,
a door hangs, hinge pinched,

its knotted wood scarred
with ax-chop memories.

Outside, feet pass
like drifting leaves,

seedless voices
strike concrete,

robins' wings
fluster the apple stump.

These Birds

You do not like these birds. They fly
like all the others. Barn, ground, trees
accept their touch, only to give it up
as birds take flight,
tossed up like seed for the gods
to grow clouds or sunlight—
wings brushing sky we cannot reach or see.

I say, my dear husband-to-be,
celebrate birds: seeds free
of earth's erratic sleep, seeds
not bound to soil and water only.
Trust the sky, where a cardinal blooms
in its blue, where she separates
from her mate, breaking gravity's restraints.

I would not rescue the red pulse
revealed beneath her wings,
reaching the single larger body—
nor would I rescue any sky
carelessly blue alive in these birds.

The Nearest While

Charged from the stratosphere,
an off-leash German shepherd
bolts towards me and my pups.
He just wants to play,
the smiling owner says.

Does he not see my arms' tautness,
my half-smile muted
by the guerrilla war escalating
between the leashes in my hands,
my unsure steps,
my face ridged like the Sierra Nevada,
dry as our southern California floor,
splitting into tiny fissures
and their still smaller off-spring, as we speak?

Not to mention my willowed breasts,
pointed earthward,
where in the relatively near future
in time's great landscape,
this body will go to reinvent itself—

doesn't he know that even his skin,
layered like ancient travelers' tales,
is dying off to make room
for new life within—
but only for the nearest while.

Fritz

As I walk one pup,
thinking I'm walking
the other one, too,

wind nudges a leaf
immeasurably green,
then a wild rose petal,
nodding calmly,
wafting its heaven scent
affirming the invisible,

one petal of one rose,
its depth of red, its burning
alliance with the sun,
stop-signing me,
its center, ovule, stamens,
pistol, petals, no less
than its own galaxy—

one rose I hold
like the last I'll ever know,
with the memory
of my loving Fritz,
put to sleep in my arms
last night,

the ghost tug
on the absent leash
of thirteen years' walking,
his littermate, Killian,
pawing the fertile ground,
wagging me into awareness
of all that makes this day beautiful.

Witness

Perched by the picture window,
the old woman ponders modern cars
flowing down the road,

interspersed with memories
of horse-drawn carriages
and Model T's,

in-betweens born of the tryst
of muscle, machine, genius,
and luck—

Come, she says, *quickly.*
What mimics a black coverlet
tossed across the lawn

is hundreds of starlings
mining the buried riches
beneath every grass blade

bathed with recent rain,
soft drops coaxing the soil
to widen its sacrificial offering

of unwitting creatures
creeping up to sunlight,
a feast in easy reach.

In her eighty-seven years,
she has witnessed
earth turn to pavement,

slide-rule to computer,
Icarus to United Airlines,
but her eye is still drawn to this:

a bounty of avian neighbors
brightening our lawn
whose ease in flight

we can only imitate
with tons of metal
and combustion.

Where We Find Ourselves

We find ourselves in the stream
pulsing on sunlit stones,

rivulets parting,
reconfiguring, merging,

variants of Earth's age-old tale
of water finding its way to the sea.

Our thoughts waft, too, ancients' breath
moving through us like sleep.

We are traces of rainbow, cloud,
mist, snow and rain,

marrow, saliva and blood—
every way water touches the earth.

We find ourselves in sleep,
drifting like islands

in unfathomed deeps, roaming
roads intriguing as unmet friends,

till wheels jam, the wagon falters,
tin cans, tools, letters,

faces, fall away like husks.
When we finally reach ourselves,

colors dance our lids like northern lights
greening and purpling the night.

We find ourselves in friends,
the collective of light

illuminating each island's place
in the all-encompassing sea,

each draws us toward
still another journey,

even deeper
than a handshake or kiss,

through constellations
of neighbors, friends, family,

fellow wayfarers
in the cosmic breath

sustaining our blue planet,
high into the heavens,

when something in us
becomes forever,

one with stars'
births and deaths,

one with their light
and dust.

Notes

"Twins" is written for my twin, Phyllis Repicky.

"Xylophones of Broken Glass" is dedicated to my late uncle, Robert MacDonald, a fan of late-night talk show host Steve Allen.

"Strains of Light" is inspired by Ryan Marlowe, poet, photographer, and protector of earth's creatures.

"*Axis Mundi*" is based on the Australian Aboriginal beliefs known as The Dreaming.

"A Poet Going Blind" is dedicated to Ruth Stone, beloved teacher and poet extraordinaire.

"Mountain Stream" pays tribute to my mother.

"Our Neck of the Woods" is inspired by Jean Ritchie. The Bluebird Song offers Ritchie's own account of the most beautiful thing she ever saw.

"Enough Music to Dance By" is dedicated to my nieces: Allison Paul; Kimberly Fox and Bailey Faldzinski; Erin, Haley, and Kayla Maffia; Heather, Lilliana, Emelia, and Juliette Kane.

"In the Somewhere Somehow Somewhen" is dedicated to my nephews: Brady Faldzinski; and Brett, Kyle, Ryan, and Eric Denby.

"New Parents" was written for Dean and Gail Borgman.

"No Discovery Without Music" is dedicated to Barry Childs, SF folk musician.

"Sailing Mission Bay" was written for Paul Repicky.

About the Author

Priscilla Denby is a writer and painter who taught English for over twenty-five years. She studied poetry under Ruth Stone at Indiana University, where she won the Academy of American Poets First Prize and earned an MA in Writing and a PhD in Folklore. Her poetry has appeared in *Poetry Northwest, Indiana Writes, Tiny Seed Journal,* and elsewhere. She grew up in Yonkers, in the shadow of New York City, and now lives in California.

Her website is:
priscilladenby.com

www.ingramcontent.com/pod-product-compliance
Lightning Source LLC
Chambersburg PA
CBHW030910170426
43193CB00009BA/802